Let's Experience Design

EXPER

TENCE

Publishers of Architecture, Art, and Design
Gordon Goff: Publisher

www.oroeditions.com
info@oroeditions.com

Published by ORO Editions

10 9 8 7 6 5 4 3 2 1 First Edition

Library of Congress data available upon
request. World Rights: Available

Graphic Design: Caroline Chua, May Chua,
Mark De Winne, Stefanie Fong.
Typograhy & Art Direction: Mark De Winne
Illustrations: Mark Wee
Editorial & Production Supervision: Joanne Tan
Writer: Adib Jalal
Additional Writing: Daniel Ye
Proofreaders: Sian Jay, Daniel Ye.
Colour Separations & Printing: Demand Print
Printed in Singapore.

International Distribution: www.oroeditions.
com/distribution

This book was printed and bound using
a variety of sustainable manufacturing
processes and materials including soy-based
inks, aqueous-based varnish, VOC- and
formaldehyde-free glues, and phthalate-free
lamninations. The text is printed using offset
sheetfed lithographic printing process on
150gsm Maple Snow paper.

ORO Editions makes a continuous effort
to minimize the overall carbon footprint of
its publications. As part of this goal, ORO
Editions, in association with Global ReLeaf,
arranges to plant trees to replace those used
in the manufacturing of the paper produced
for its books. Global ReLeaf is an international
campaign run by American Forests, one of
the world's oldest nonprofit conservation
organizations. Global ReLeaf is American
Forests' education and action program that
helps individuals, organizations, agencies,
and corporations improve the local and global
environment by planting and caring for trees.

Design!

MARK WEE & KEN YUKTASEVI
ONG&ONG EXPERIENCE DESIGN STUDIO

It's hard to define experience design. As Patrick Newbury, Chief Strategy Officer at Method, said in a WIRED magazine article[1], "Experience design is not a checklist, a recipe, or a series of manoeuvers; it is a way of thinking." We agree.

Experience design is in everything we do . From paying for our groceries to communicating with our family, every interaction, every device and every object we touch was designed by someone. The materials, the order of the spaces, and the form of things were all specified by a designer. In this light, everything we experience is designed.

Most people are drawn towards rich and well-designed experiences. The creation of these experiences cannot be careless; it must be thoughtful. It requires new ways of thinking— thinking that embraces multi-dimensional perspectives, unfamiliar systems, empathy and rigorous testing. Creating rich experiences should not be the job of designers alone. Everyone can be in the business of creating delightful memories for others.

Perhaps you are a chef. Maybe a writer or a civil servant. If you're in the business of serving others and want to make experiences just a little more thoughtful and enjoyable, this book is for you. We wrote it to demystify the thinking process behind this field of experience design.

This book dives into the 5-steps of the Experience Design process we undertake in the studio. Each step gets its own chapter. Apart from sharing our values and philosophy, we tell stories of how we applied the process. To help you along, we offer simple pointers we have picked up along the way that you can use in your own projects.

We hope this book inspires you to create many delightful, designed experiences.

—

¹ *Experience Design: When Innovation Isn't Enough | WIRED*, http://www.wired.com/2014/03/experience-design-innovation-isnt-enough/ (accessed June 01, 2015).

THE BUSINESS OF

SOME TIME IN THE LATER HALF OF 2014, the global architecture industry went into a self-reflective debate after Pritzker-prize winning architect, Frank Gehry, declared at a press conference that 98% of everything that is built and designed today has "no sense of design, no respect for humanity or for anything else"[1].
Gehry considered them as "buildings and nothing else," and this sparked a series of op-eds in key architectural journals with many suggesting that the architecture profession is failing[2].

While some may be drawn to subscribe to this perceived downfall, we like to think that this is instead a moment of opportunity for the rise of a more relevant and holistic way to design.

Here at ONG&ONG, we believe that good design is experienced through various multi-sensorial touchpoints and therefore, we are in the business of designing delightful experiences in the built environment. We achieve this through our complete 360° solution which offers a cross-discipline approach. A key part of this is the employment of a design thinking methodology in the design process.

Through this structured and deliberate process, we are able to uncover deep knowledge and insights into the user's needs, allowing us to innovate entirely new and meaningful spatial experiences. Going beyond architectural services, this forms part of a completely new value chain in design that enables the creation of not just a tangible end product, but also intangible experiences and emotions that run deeper.

TAI LEE SIANG,
GROUP MANAGING DIRECTOR
ONG & ONG

EXPERIENCES

The 5-stage Experience Design process is a fascinating idea-driven and human-centric journey and we truly believe in its power to transform the way we experience and design our environments. We hope that by sharing more about how we design experiences in this book, we can inspire and empower the many other creative minds like yourself to do the same, and together we can experience even more delightful designs in our daily lives.

———

[1] Stephen Burgen, *Frank Gehry gives journalist the finger | The Guardian*, http://www.theguardian.com/artanddesign/2014/oct/24/frank-gehry-journalist-finger-architecture-shit (accessed June 01, 2015).

[2] Justin Shubow, *Architecture Continues To Implode: More Insiders Admit The Profession Is Failing | Forbes.com,* http://www.forbes.com/sites/justinshubow/2015/01/06/architecture-continues-to-implode-more-insiders-admit-the-profession-is-failing/ (accessed June 01, 2015).

IN 2009, THE ECONOMIC STRATEGIES COMMITTEE cast a vision for Singapore to be a 'Highly Skilled People, Innovation Economy, and Distinctive Global City' in our next lap of growth, and presented strategies for the nation to maximize our opportunities in a new world environment. An ambitious goal was set to increase productivity by 2-3% over the next ten years, and to do this, a clear shift to growth that was based on skills, innovation, and productivity was identified. With the world facing increasingly complex problems and its existing systems experiencing rapid change, much of our technical knowledge and products are quickly becoming redundant. We as a people and nation now need innovative new solutions that can be integrated into all aspects of society and business for us to handle the many new opportunities and challenges in the years to come.

Creativity will be key in enabling us to maximize new opportunities, and to find the most productive responses to challenge. Design thinking will be a key problem-solving tool to address these existing and future issues – it being an iterative process that generates ideas, transforms them, and presents them in realities. The new Dsg-II Blueprint for Design for Singapore outlines a vision for design thinking to be taught and integrated into all levels of society in the next 5 to 10 years and I believe that we are at the start of a historical journey towards, quite possibly, the world's first Design Thinking Nation.

Why and what is design thinking? Design thinking is essentially the process of thought and action that designers use towards the crafting of new experiences or systems that address the user's needs. It is a powerful innovation tool that embraces a highly exploratory and multi-dimensional perspective towards problem solving through immersion and empathy, a discipline of rigorous testing, and looking to make associations and connections across fields of discipline and industry for inspiration and solutions. This emergent way of systems thinking greatly contrasts with traditional linear thinking that privileges the planning of a flawless intellect, is adverse to failure, relies on expert advantage, and arms length research. In many

DESIGNING EXPERIENCES

MARK WEE, DIRECTOR, EXPERIENCE DESIGN

ways, one could generalize that though traditional thinking was important in addressing the problems in the old world, design thinking is necessary to tackle the problems in our new world. It is at the heart of this that Singapore hopes to prepare herself to tackle her new world.

I was trained and still practice today as an architect. Although the traditional scope of my profession is centered about the building of physical human environments in architecture and interiors, I have always understood the potential of design outside its traditional disciplines. It is my belief that a rigorous design education shapes the mind with the ability to understand problems and visualize new solutions spatially. As designers create new products, services, or environments that ultimately sit within an existing context of needs and wants, they naturally develop a systems thinking approach to problem solving and solution. The strength and ability of this skill are, I believe, in many ways determined by the type and rigour of their design education. This skill, if embraced in interdisciplinary teams and applied towards analyzing problems and issues, offers a fresh, dynamic approach to innovation.

In Pine & Gilmore's seminal book 'The Experience Economy' in 1999, the authors prophetically outlined a future economic offering based on experiences over that of the service economy. Tracing the history of the traditional economic offerings of commodities, goods, and services, we are shown how in this service economy, customers are now increasingly valuing services more highly than just goods based on price and availability.

As a result, manufacturers often deliver services as bundles with their core goods to provide fuller, more robust economic offerings to satisfy their customers' needs. An example of this would be telecommunication providers that offer a huge discount to the purchase of a mobile phone in conjunction with an increasing length of mobile service packages. Even then, services are also becoming increasingly commoditized as witnessed in the price wars in areas of the airline industry through budget carriers such as AirAsia. Likewise, financial services such as E-trade, and internet based services such as Skype and Whatsapp that directly compete with telecommunication providers with free calls and messaging, also form part of this trend. Clearly, with the Internet being one of the greatest forces of commoditization that allow us instant price comparisons for services and goods across the world, companies can now connect directly with their end buyers, circumventing traditional middlemen.

With all this, a new emerging economy is coming to the fore, one based on a distinctive kind of economic output – that of experiences. Experiences are events that engage individuals in a personal way, leaving a memory and impression. Evidence of this importance is seen in the popularity of travel guides such as the Lonely Planet that furnish us with information to experience a destination authentically and Travel & Leisure and other lifestyle periodicals that feature the best 'vacation experiences around the world'. The world's most successful manufacturers of goods focus on the experiences that their customers have while using their goods, such as the interface design experience of an Apple product, and the ability to train with your friend or run with thousands across the world with the Nike+Running technology series. This is signifying a fundamental shift from a traditional focus of design on how a product performs, to that of the user and how the individual performs while using the good. It is with this new focus that design thinking can be an invaluable tool for innovation and success in this new experience economy.

It is with this conviction at ONG&ONG Experience Design that we approach design and the creation of experiences that people will love. We understand that great experiences are a responsible and yet imaginative combination of products, services, and the environment. In a world where the successful design practice is often defined by its stars or the large corporations, and where the media often celebrates the provocative image over that of how well it has served its user, it is opportune time for change and a different way of practice.
We believe that it is time for a practice that will place the user needs above the sake of the designer's statement, a celebration of the interdisciplinary team over that of the sole genius designer, and a culture of honour over selfish ambition.

In the last few years, we have had the privilege of havinga great team of passionate individuals work alongside us in this mission, all bound by a common passion to serve our users, make meaningful work in this world, and, of course, to provide a personal experience to them. This curiosity and openness to what design could do have led us into the fields of research, branding, education and training, and strategy and consulting, outside our core sphere of built environments. We have realized that being able to empathize with others, a desire to truly understand their needs, and the willingness to share and work alongside them is an approach that is invaluable in tackling any problem.

As Singapore makes its shift towards becoming what I believe will be the world's first design thinking economy, I am excited, as it signifies a journey of discovery for us to also find our heart as we strive to carve a relevant place for ourselves in this world.

----

[1] Joseph Pine & James Gilmore, *The Experience Economy,* 1999, pg. 9-15

Your breath being taken away when you see the forest for the first time on your holiday to Kyoto.

Getting from bed to the supermarket and paying for the groceries.

Eating your favorite comfort food with the people you love around you.

The way you communicate with your family.

WHAT DO ALL THESE MOMENTS HAVE IN COMMON?
DESIGN.

Now more than ever, the above experiences will be influenced, enhanced and enabled by the presence of intentional design. What we eat will be brought to our tables from farms and kitchens that have been optimized for maximum productivity, efficiency and customer experience. Our cities' living and transport will have been planned using drones and big data so we can get to work as quickly and as happily as possible. We would have found that forest in Kyoto, snapped a photo and shared it with our community using the device that is less than a meter away from you as you read this.

EXPERIENCING DESIGN

KEN YUKTASEVI.
DIRECTOR, EXPERIENCE DESIGN

As spaces, places and things become connected over the next five years, you will see a crumbling of the walls between graphic designers, technologists, interface designers, and so on. As life becomes more designed, design will become more a part of life.

For a moment, let's kill our current understanding of the faculty of design and its disciplines. A good way to experience the essence of something is to try stripping it back so you can truly taste and see it for what it is. As you read this book, suspend any solid definitions of design. Instead, behold design's tangible effects on how people relate to each other and to life itself. Yes we dare say it: let's get spiritual about experiencing design.

Still here? Thank you for being open minded, you've already started to experience design. There is a powerful interpretation of scripture that reads,

> *"Let us make human beings in our image, make them reflecting our nature, so they can be responsible for the fish in the sea, the birds in the air, the cattle, and, yes, Earth itself."*

Christians believe that God's intended design is for humans to reflect Him, and that in turn puts a responsibility on us. A responsibility where what we design will inevitably reflect us.

This book is not just for the designers; it is for moms, teachers, chefs, students, politicians, and doctors. In short, it is for people. In order for design to take its place as servant to a better life, everyone needs to experience design.

IDEATE 3

PROTOTYPE 4

5 DESIGN

VERY

Unveiling Truth

The first ingredient
to experiencing
meaningful design is
to embrace 'truth'.
Without this,
everything we create
will not amount to
anything important
or significant.

The experience design journey begins with finding out the truth. We do our best work when we have a comprehensive understanding of the design problem.

However, nothing is as straightforward as it seems. There are historical layers to peel away, implied meanings to decipher, familiar routines to learn, insider knowledge to discover, and bureaucracy to navigate. The prize is valuable insight that can inform the radical transformation of an experience.

In the *Discovery* process, one approaches the work with a mix of Jedi awareness, child-like curiosity and Sherlockian deduction. At this early stage, the insights we get are as good as the questions we ask. The best questions always come from the people we are designing for – the end users and our clients. Armed with the right questions, the designer then leans in to listen and observe, reading between the lines for gems that reveal what really matters.

INTERVIEWS

GROUP INTERVIEWS.

EXTREME & MAINSTREAM USERS

SECONDARY RESEARCH

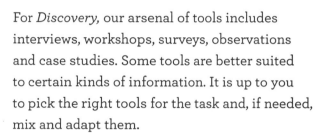

For *Discovery,* our arsenal of tools includes
interviews, workshops, surveys, observations
and case studies. Some tools are better suited
to certain kinds of information. It is up to you
to pick the right tools for the task and, if needed,
mix and adapt them.

Here are examples of how we applied the
Discovery process to our projects.

SINGAPORE BOTANIC GARDENS SHOPS

SBG

LOW COST TO ENTER NOG.

CAME SPECIFICALLY FOR THE ORCHID GARDEN

WE ENJOYED MBS TOO. WOULD STILL RECOMMEND SBG/NOG

GOT LOST IN THE SBG - CONFUSING

Takes photos to be encapsulate his experience at BG.

- WOULD LOVE TO HAVE A DOG PARK.
- DESIGNATED DOG RUN.

WOULD LIKE TO LEAVE FEELING HAPPY.

SBG RETAINS GREENERY THAT IS BEING LOST IN SINGAPORE. REFUGE FROM BUSY LIFE
- SBG is like a sanctuary in SG.
- Space to enjoy & chill.

♡ GREENERY, PEACEFUL, FLORA, FAUNA SPACE

LOVED THE LAYOUT OF THE SBG. UNIQUE

I feel quite boxed up in botanical gardens. cuz surrounding it are like roads & concretes

I had fond memories of e old botanical gardens during kindergarten!

It was just diff I guess? Break e daily routine of concrete blocks & school.

being there with mum was def a plus!

Most impressive
- mix of different environments
- orderly
- infinite number

what's unique?
- It's quite empty compared to other gardens
- (coz weekday)
- Entrance fee stopped them for going into NoG.
- Love the variety of different atmospheres

Hard to access different parts of the park. Would like it to be more accessible. (esp. by car)

More concerts & events would be nice & to get more people to the SBG.

- There should be art classes to teach pple how to sketch nature & plants.
- Didn't know that

Wish there'll be more shady areas & flatter land for jogging.

- Want it more to be more SG.
  - eg. Laksa tasting event.
  - eat local food & enjoy local music.
- Classes to teach how to grow local plants
- Horticultural classes.

GIFTING

THOUGHT BEHIND GIFT IS MORE IMPT. GIFT ITSELF CAN BE SECONDARY

DOESN'T FIND GIFTS FROM GIFT SHOP MEANINGFUL

I like to think that every souvenir I get had some thought put to it.

WHY BUY GIFTS
- because there's an occasion.
- one of the languages of love.
- to express love / care for the person.
- something green
- take away e different experiences with the pple / food.
- gives her perspective and her curiosity discovery.

DON'T CARE ABOUT THE GIFT SHOPS.

RETAIL SHOPS / GIFT SHOPS
- Buy souvenirs for basic courtesy.
  - no sentimental connects
  - useless
- Never been to the gift shops at the gardens.
- Would love to buy seeds of local plants
- Not advertised enough.

GIFTS / SOUVENIRS
- do v. rarely buy souvenirs/ gifts 'coz cliché
- need to be authentic & or artistic eg. saffron from Egypt. dates
- If I buy, it'll have to fit into my bag and functional.
- Don't buy stuff for family / friends.
- Would bring foodstuff mostly

BEST GIFT
- Samy: uncle went to Bali and brought back a boat/sarik for him.
- Made him feel special & that his uncle remembered him on the trip.

How do you like to remember travel experiences?
- memories & funny stories. (eg. Greece)
- Journal / Diary
- Drawing
- Rem. People

Perfect gift for someone else
- my time for the person.
- A good vacation for myself.
- discover another
- makes her a happier person
- ultimately, being a blessing to others by being blessed. (a trip is a blessing to her.)

- Would buy local produce.
- anything edible is a useful / practical gift.

LOCAL PRODUCE (AT LEAST FROM ASIA)

GOOD FOR GIVING TO FOREIGN FRIEND
- thought the shops sold generic souvenirs like the Merlion so didn't bother

USER
INTERVIEWS

CAN W
PLEAS
ESCAPE
THE HEA

TOURIST

SG Re

♡ AUTHEN
GIFTS.
ie. ORCHID

NATURE

Is nature (not pt to you)

- Yes 'coz I love
going to parks &
outdoors.
- A bit tough in
SG 'coz it's so
hot.

LOVE ORCHID
RELATED
SOUVENIRS

DON'T LIKE
BEING
PRESSURED
TO BUY
GIFTS

GIFT DOESN'T
HAVE TO
BE EXPENSIV
JUST
MEANINGFUL

Exp. nature in SG

In fresh & shaded
environment
w/ Ice Kachang
At the entrance
and exit w/ chendo
why is that represent
- Exp. local plants
- little night safari
exp.
- on a path & explore
local plants
- a little history
- old Drama...

eg. Melbourne by
Foot 'tour.
- throw in local
delights.
- Culture, arts &
food.

- Loves botany
- Attempts to
upkeep the
garden at home

How to connect to
nature?
- Visually relaxes
you.
- Relaxation aspect.
- To get your day
started.
- Looking at greenery

CRAIG

IND. TOURIST
GDN ENTUSIAST
EXPAT

DAVID +

DO

SUJATA
&
SAMY

R

DOESN'T BUY
GIFTS TO
SUMMARIZE
HIS EXP.

valuable
exp.

What does the idea
e gdn mean to you?
Cooking
mainly herbs &
ingredients you use
to
Mt. Tomah cook.
- plants from all
over e world
you can see the love
and care that has
gone into taking of
the garden / plants

Best gift?
prolly a tribal
necklace, nth
fancy but
represented his
view of me as
a person.
everyone likes a
free gift, and
it's impt cuz
it tells e person
you thought of
them while
you were away

♡ Amazing
landscapes,
spectacular sunset
golden beaches —
e list goes on!

- Reminded her of
God's love for her.
If someone can take
care of the plants
with so much caree
love, how much
more does God take
care of her. 😊

1. SHEEP
eg. Chinese T.
coach bus
package
business travel
impomm day-tou

I'd bring food
back if that's
not possible
then some random
souvenirs meant
e most for a
particular trip

But theres def
more to that.
I also enjoy e
idea of challenge
and risk being
outdoors.
Enjoy nature?
simple as having
a BBQ with
friends at a park
or cycling throug
e park
connector.

Aesthetics is
def one of e
reason why I
enjoy being
outdoors!

Pulau Ubin was
where I exp
nature at
it's best!
that quarry
was amazing.
Would like to exp.
nature in sg
in wilderness
but there are
def pockets of
nature that
everyone should exp.

Needs ①

remember trip
②

⑤ express
care + live fo
those of know

Founded in 1859 as a public park, the Singapore Botanic Gardens is one of the oldest in Southeast Asia, boasting a collection of more than 1000 plant species and 2000 orchid hybrids. It represents the biodiversity of the region. Singaporeans are proud of it. Recently, it underwent a massive upgrading programme and drew over 3 million local and foreign visitors who came to enjoy the main garden and other attractions—the Ginger, Orchid, Evolution, Children's and Healing Gardens as well as the Heritage, Rain Forest and Evolution Trails. In addition to these attractions, the Gardens wanted to enhance the experience through retail offerings that would address the needs of the garden users and make the Gardens more meaningful and memorable.

We believed that the Gardens meant different things to different people. By employing a variety of *Discovery* techniques, we hoped to have as complete a picture as possible. We conducted site studies, interviews, online surveys and also used our "Donut method" to look at retail experiences from around the world to have a better understanding of the landscape.

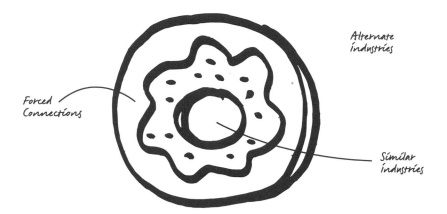

Forced
Connections

Alternate
industries

Similar
industries

Working with the staff at the shops, we engaged
tour guides, tourists, customers at the shops and
selected visitors at the Botanic Gardens. One-on-
one interviews helped us get in-depth responses
while online surveys provided us with a broader
view of visitor sentiment.

We sleuthed out underlying desires and emotions
expressed in statements like "I would like to be
comfortable in nature - without sweat, unhurried,
unforced but yet feels [sic] natural". Responses
like this can spark a variety of ideas .

this is'nt the donut you're looking for

TEABAR

rt
rt. wallet

ONLINE SURVEY

MEANING OF SBG	LOVELY OASIS CLEAN LUSH	FELT CLOSE TO NATURE, FELT SUPR SURPRISED BY GREENERY	QUIETNESS SPACE TO DO MANY THINGS	ALLOWS PEOPLE TO FELLOWSHIP & RELAX	THE PROTECT TREES THE CACTUS GARDEN
BETTER SBG	MORE F&B more accessible	MORE MAPS around the path junctions	MORE EVENTS, MORE SHELTER	MORE TOILETS	GET RID RESTAURA & STORES
HOW SBG RATES AS SG ATTRACT BRAND	NBG SPECIAL UNIQUE TO SG, NBG SPECIAL yes.	SBG SHOULD FIRST BE TOP ATTRACT TO LOCALS — eg MEAN SOMETHG TO US.	NEEDS TO TELL A STORY, CANNOT JUST BE A PLACE TO LEARN ABOUT PLANTS.	NOTHING UNIQUE OR else I dont know about it.	NET STIMU FOR TOURIS MORE A PL TO UNWIN
REMEMBER SBG	ORCHID AS MEMENTO ORCHID VENEZUALA IN A JAR - I COLLECT JARS.	· FALLEN LEAVES, · A FLOWER, · FLOWERS, · A FLOWER PRESS	_ SWAN FEATHER _ A WATER-LILY _ A LEAF	£ -PRESSED FLOWER, - ORCHID PETALS	A small potted ov £1
NATURE	GREEN, PEACEFUL ESCAPE FROM CITY	PICNIC W FAMILY & FRIENDS	RAW & UNTOUCHED DON'T TRY TO HARD TO CREATE	NATURE AS PURE, UNTOUCHED LIKE A WHOLE NEW WORLD	IN A CAR A GOOD A RUNN EVEN
REMEMBER TRAVEL BY	BUY SOMETHING UNIQUE & PRECIOUS SIGNATURE mementoes — eg. snowglobes figurines painting	REPRESENTS THE PLACE making new friends	SOMETHING FROM THE PLACE EG. SAND FROM BEACH.	PARTICIPATING IN EVENTS connecting with people — relationships that are unforgettable	_ A NICE _ UNIQUE _ GREAT F
WHAT GIFT YOU BUY?	CAN'T GET ANYWHERE ELSE	- USEFUL TO DAILY LIFE, - A DESK ACCESSORY	1) MUST REFLECT E PLACE 2) PERSONAL TO E RECIPIENT.	- A PAINTING	ACCESSO Light &
BEST GIFT YOU'VE RECEIVED	BEAUTIFUL HANDMADE FROM JAPAN Fabric, textile — useful & durable Pebble from famous pebble beach in Taiwan	MUG FROM LONDON W MY NAME — WENT OUT OF WAY 2 GET	RED CIRCLE SHADES FROM VINTAGE SHOP IN LONDON. 1) I ♥ LONDON 2) I ♥ GLASSES 3) I ♥ VINTAGE	A small toy - mic that my friend took the time to look for something unique, thats suitable for my character	A bag. Hi special I always y for it

· "product material sourced from gardens." · SG orchids? body lotion

Specialty retailer and ... general ... professional ... creating ...

· SBG NOT is our origins! unthinkable not to be there.

· "Our designs are inspired by NATURE"

... shop ... like cutting Rather be designer &

Child in a candy store Everything is ...

the Singaporean's concept of nature is a dichotomy between
a) raw, original, unpunched
b) clean, comfortable, ... sweat-free

GIFT
... reflects the time & thought the giver
... is compatible & personal to the recipient

young people today value the personal, ... experiential and unique more than ... material & ... monetary value of the gift "... FACTOR"

People want different things in the souvenirs they buy for themselves vs those they buy for others

SBG to b sing ma an

- ~~UNIQUE FOOD~~ HERITAGE TREES DUCK-FEEDING

- VARIETY OF FLORA + FAUNA

- BIG & CLEAN

- DISTINCT + DIFFERENT FROM CITY. GREEN, SPACIOUS

- THE HERITAGE OF THE PLACE — COLONIAL, YET TROPICAL

- Waterfall, the layout of gardens the pavilions

- pristine Lush, no two views the same

- More outdoor furniture: swings — hammocks — that surprise people

- More natural views, less manufactured

- FANS w/ mist

- No. SG is a shopper's paradise. SBG has nothing. SBG is not uniquely Singaporean.

- GARDENS BY THE BAY IS MUCH BETTER GARDENS BY THE BAY HAS MORE HYPE

- PREFER SBG to GARDENS BY BAY — more natural.

- NOT as attractive to younger crowd as orchard Rd or even sentosa — cannot compete

- More a place to relax & rest, not a tourist attraction

- LOCAL FOODS YES, IT REPRESENTS "GARDEN CITY"

- YES, its a unique experience. Yes, cos its been there since beginning + no touristy shops. Yes, its a familiar, historical icon

- IT'S QU... BORIN... AN ATTRA... NOT M... "WOW... FACT... NOTHI... INTERE... ABOU... MUSE... AIR CON...

- ...ed plant, terrarium

- ...ower

- Live orchid plant

- Gardens about plants — I want to cultivate something of my own at home

- Something I can grow eg seedling —

- WANT NATURE TO BE INFUSED INTO CITY LIFE

- SIT ON GRASS & NOT BE AFRAID OF DIRT

- BY BICYCLE ORIGINAL, UNTOUCHED

- LEARN MORE abt flora + fauna – native? – edible?

- more activities – do something amongst nature

- In comfort, without sweat unhurried, unforced.

- Look well-maintained but natural eg Dutch flower fields or Japanese sakura season

- –A KEYCHAIN –MAPS just experiences. & thats intangible

- –BY TWEETING – A SMELL

- – ~~THE FOODS,~~ –THE SERVICE, –THINGS TO DO THERE

- something I can keep or display so it reminds me of the experience

- A SOUVENIR THAT SPEAKS BEST ABT THE COUNTRY'S CULTURE

- the place BOOKS abt the place.

- A 3D paper cutting of the garden.

- –A LOCAL SPECIALTY

- _AUTHENTIC FOOD RECIPES – LOCAL FOODS – WINE – FOOD

- PLUCK A FLOWER.

- Small but useful eg. bookmark or cup.

- something one-of-a-kind

- HANDCRAFTED SOUVENIR, cultural essence of the country

- PIECE OF ART FROM THAT COUNTRY earrings from Australia — made from coral.

- PHOTOBOOK OF MEMORIES ~~SNOW~~ SNOWGLOBES A bag of a lot of things from that country — showed variety & thought when person bought it.

- LOCAL ALCOHOL— LOCAL FOOD Food that can't be found in SG. A swarovski nail-filer from Prague — pretty yet practical.

- A POSTCARD from OVERSEAS featuring local architecture

- A RUSSIAN USHANKA (fur hat), cos u can't find them here.

- TEA, it was super fragrant -Books, postcards - miniatures I enjoy unique knowledge + adventure

- A shirt from Egypt — special cos it had Egyptian writing on it

- the shops SBG & hence the shops need to offer something for everyone, not at every location

- heritage site, s... needs to shar... story to a global audience — & the shops are garden part of that story

- ...s of wealth, ...ths, ...s according ...

But story can be an authentic ~~relevant~~ embraced by ALL

- SBG's story is about singapore's roots. — ~~we are~~ its about knowing who we are — first a untamed jungle ⟶ to a cultivated garden

- requires c... commitment, dedication. there are no accidental gardens

Engaging visitors and users in *Discovery* gave us much useful information for the later phases of our experience design process. We created user personas with a studied spread of motivations and needs. We imagined narratives for the shops and its patrons and created an experience the visitor would remember and cherish.

These are just glimpses into how we do *Discovery*. While we have our own methods, you are the expert in your field. The *Discovery* tools we use can be easily adapted for your own use.

HDB PUNGGOL BRANCH

PUNGGOL BRANCH

Why Q when you can do it anywhe...

STATION 1

SCANNER BOOTH

STATION 2

THE Housing & Development Board (HDB) wanted to set up a new Branch in Punggol that would better serve the needs of the residents in Punggol Town. This new Branch was an opportunity to re-think the customer service experience at a typical branch and to adopt a user-centric approach in designing the office layout and delivery of Branch services. Our brief was to create an experience that would help HDB staff deliver Branch services more seamlessly and to give customers a warm and personable touch as they went through the various touch points.

Before we could start designing a new experience, we spent time discovering to get a fuller grasp of the overall context. This went beyond the usual and obvious spatial requirements and included a deeper understanding of why people went to the Branch Office and how they went about their business.

home
e years to live and repent
LET ME SIT!
T online
to visit
status
unit
new ga
Shimmering with
x number of car
$1.4b tower coming up on historical parking site
a wall of worry
one of the greatest bull runs in history
Gallery
DB
Discover Singapore's Public Housing Story
HOUSING DEVELOPMENT BOARD
slums to vibrant towns
80%
HOUSING & DEVELOPMENT BOARD
world.international
Pregna
linke
MY NAME IS

Senior Managem

① – Service Centres
at leading ed
service indus
held in esteem
govt and prive

② Different stro
different folk
BOs designed f
of estate
eg. → face-to
→ high-
3e4

No one

③ BOs as social hub for residents
to bond
eg. venue for welcome parties
– provide compelling
reason for residents to
visit.

④ Re-define relationship
between BO & residents.
eg. specific CSOs mobile
to attend to residents
needs – can visit at
home or offices
like banks' relationship
managers.
BOs as satellite
places for face-to-fa
necessary
self-help

on deserted
obstruction
– EPS parking

CP lot
d to queue
o transac on
phone
lot basis
re lots!
ding system
ns/e-alerts
n availability
ive updates
borderless
underground parking
link bridges

LIVING   DINING

PUBLIC

BEDROOM
TOILET
PRIVATE

¿

We began this process by setting out to under-stand the purpose of this HDB Branch—not its stated purpose, but an actual user-centric design brief. We analysed the transactions that took place over a few months and discovered distinct patterns. We explored the reasons for these patterns and how we could come up with a strategy to better meet customers' needs by paying more attention to the little experiences surrounding those transactions. We kept this in mind as we dug deeper.

To understand why people visited the Branch, we conducted a series of interviews and surveys with staff and customers. If most transactions could be done online, why did people visit the Branch? Were there common motivations among the customers? If so, could design enhance the experience of these customers? Could we help the staff serve their customers better?

On a mission to discover more, we spent days immersed in the space and the psyche of those who used it. Our interviews with staff and customers included questions about the physical environment, communication methods, and work processes. We watched staff and customers use the space and found challenges common to both. No detail was too small as we set out to identify critical environmental touchpoints that affected the customer experience in a typical Branch environment.

Discovery for this project did not only cover a breadth of topics and stakeholders. It also helped us understand unspoken desires and motivations. As we took time to interact with the people and space, we began to see the possiblity of richer design solutions beyond the intent outlined in the project brief.

Touchpoints are a dynamic way of breaking down and mapping out an experience to help everyone understand it and engage with it.

OUR
DISCOVERY
TOOLS

Here at the ONG&ONG Experience Design Studio, we use different tools to draw out different types of insights. Some tools are more suitable for certain types of information. It is really up to you to choose how to use them. Mix them up and adapt them as you see fit for your project. Who knows what you will find?

INTERVIEWS

Interviews are an excellent way to gather in-depth understanding of end-users, staff and other stakeholders.

One-to-one interviews are perfect for developing a deep understanding of the people we design for. The key is to pick interview subjects ranging over a wide spectrum of users and staff. Through these personal sessions that can take anything from a few minutes to over an hour, we build a good rapport and gather insights into their motivations, dreams and stories. From these, we distill real needs.

Impromptu interviews are done when we conduct observational site studies and are a quick way to test assumptions and gain clarity. The data gathered during impromptu interviews are useful for generating statistics and getting a general sense of how people feel.

When formulating interview questions, avoid superficial questions or wishlist-type questions. If we were working on an F&B project, questions like "What do you think can be improved?" might get responses such as "there should be better air-conditioning". A response like that reveals nothing of deeper motivations. Instead, a question such as "What is your favourite restaurant experience and why?" prompts the interviewee to reveal their ideals and deeper desires. These lead to better insights and, consequently, better design.

We like interviews to feel casual. We usually conduct interviews in comfortable public places like cafés. People feel more open when relaxed! We are also cautious of responses shaped by groupthink when interviewing multiple people at a time.

Another tool that we often use in Discovery is Workshops. These are always specially designed for each project and conducted in groups ranging from 8 to 30.

The true value of running workshops is in uncovering the internal relationships and dynamics within the organization. This is an opportunity to observe the current company culture. Remember to involve various stakeholders in these sessions! Workshops are also useful for finding out the goals, fears and positioning of the company. You'll learn their perception of themselves and how they like to be perceived by their clients. All this comes in handy later in the design process.

Most of all, workshops should be fun. Encourage everyone to be open and to express themselves. A great way to do this is to create a supportive environment. Our workshops always involve a lot of drawings, doodling, markers, post-its, and laughter! Get creative with your workshop exercises and you may unearth gems of insight from the participants. There'll be examples from our projects in the later pages we hope will inspire you.

Have fun, but remember what you are trying to draw out. Document the process. Take photos, record audio and video where possible. Scan all the documents so that you have something to refer to in the later stages.

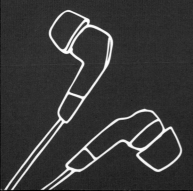

3

S U R V E Y S

In Discovery, we also use face-to-face and online surveys. Surveys are most effective when we need quick responses to simple questions that can be answered directly or by multiple- choice.

Surveys are also useful for gathering quantitative data. Often, the information we get out of these is very different from what we get from interviews and workshops, which produce more emotive and personal data.

For example, in our Discovery phase of the Gardens Shop, we asked very simple questions such as "Have you been to the Botanic Gardens before?" and "Do you think the Gardens represent Singapore's top list of attractions?". These were simple, yet meaningful. With responses from a wide range of respondents, we quickly established basic knowledge of the project and its issues.

The value of surveys is realised when the sample size is large enough to reveal trends and patterns. However, surveys are less useful in drawing out responses to complicated questions. Participants are often not as engaged when answering survey questions without someone talking to them and walking them through. They might also struggle to gain clarity on questions they don't understand.

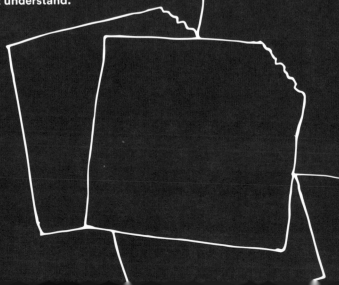

CASE STUDIES

Looking at other positive examples is also a very useful way for us to learn more about the possibilities ahead.

In these case studies, we often look for moods, programming, design, process, customer engagement, branding and any other elements of a project that we think have the potential to be translated to the brief at hand.

In the studio, we use a method called "The Donut" to search for case studies. At the centre of the donut are case studies from similar industries. This is where we identify what is being done by peers and competitors. Then, we look around at alternative industries before examining far-off industries for left-field ideas. Go forth and look for inspiration!

5

OBSERVATIONS

A humble but critical tool is site observations.
This is all about being still and gathering undisturbed
and unbiased information.

Like a well-trained secret agent, we often find an
inconspicuous and comfortable vantage point of the
area that we want to observe. In this study of the site,
we look out for the interaction of users and staff with
the space. We also observe social dynamics, how people
use the space and the real reasons people come to the
area. You may be surprised that a space may not always
be used for its intended purpose. Find out why!

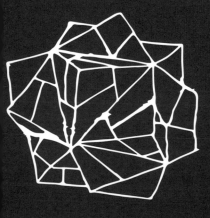

SYNT

Think like a parent

HESIS

Wisdom, love and empathy form the secret sauce which enables designers to settle on the right design problems to solve. This comes naturally to a parent.

The dust settles from *Discovery* and we are left with a hill of data waiting to be turned into knowledge. Steven Levitt, author of *Freakonomics*, said, "Go out and collect data and, [don't be afraid of not having the answer] instead of having the answer, just look at the data and see if the data tells you anything."[1]

In *Synthesis,* we make sense of raw data. This is the hardest but most important step. We cluster and distill findings. We seek patterns and themes. We turn early insights around and around like newly-cut gems, looking for an angle that unlocks a fresh way of seeing the problem. Seeing the problem in a fresh way is more likely to yield new ideas.

Sometimes, there is insufficient data to support a particular point-of-view. We aren't shy about revisiting *Discovery* for more data to confirm or disprove our assumptions. Don't fret if you have to run to and fro between stages—it's what makes experience design more honest, rigorous, and even exciting!

But how is *Synthesis* done? How does one analyse, distill and repurpose the information gathered? What's important? What's not? How can it be made useful for the following *Ideate* stage?

PORT OF LOST WONDER BY SENTOSA

Sentosa, an island resort in Singapore, boasted 18.6 million guests[2] between 2013 and 2014. One of its key attractions is Singapore's first kids' club by the beach, Port of Lost Wonders, which our studio had the privilege of helping to create. Targeted towards children aged 3 to 10 years of age, the attraction was imagined to be a signature water play area, and we helped develop the overall narrative and customer experience of the Kids' Club. It was to be located at Palawan Beach, Sentosa.

We started with *Discovery*. We engaged in deep research, conducted interviews and workshops with staff, parents, kids and "extreme users". In two weeks of *Discovery*, we also facilitated a workshop[conversations, laughter and doodling] with Sentosa's key stakeholders to come up with an ideal Kids' Club experience. By the end of the session, we had a wealth of information, ready to be mined for insights.

Extreme users help us design solutions for people at the far end of the spectrum.

Those who love organising and arranging things into tidy groups might enjoy this stage of the experience design process where we seek clarity in the mass of data. We set out to make sense of reams of transcripts and stacks of notes and collages from the engagement sessions. We analysed words with the help of tools like *Wordle*, drew diagrams in attempts to link seemingly disparate lines of thinking, and then simplifed the same diagrams further to arrive at the core issues. This act of seeking out patterns led to a few recurring fundamental ideas like the notion of assurance, where parents wanted to know that their kids would be safe on the premises and in the hands of the Club's staff. Assurance and other key ideas then became critical guidelines for the ideal experience at the Kids' Beach Club.

Child prodigy Adora Svitak shares in her TED talk[3] that grown-ups have a lot to learn from children. This project attests to that. While we looked to understand the missing ingredients in the current play experience, the youngest stakeholders of Sentosa really helped us see things clearly. For example, one of the kids had this to say during an interview: "We love surprises and gifts, like the free mints Fish & Co. leaves for every guest after their meal." This sense of delight and surprise that makes the kids feel special was simple and powerful. We worked hard to imbue our final design with it.

It was during the review of the transcripts that we were able make sense of initial reactions to the earlier pirate-themed proposal. Parents saw pirates as violent and male-oriented. Kids identified them as scary or dirty!

These findings, simple on hindsight, turned out to be very valuable. Good insights are produced by this dogged cycle of engagement and synthesis. For us, this is the value of the experience design process. It's understanding the seeds to be planted so that we may reap the great ideas that grow out of it at a later stage. This process of synthesis helped us to refine our focus and derive keywords such as Freedom, Empowerment, Bonding, Connection, Creativity and Adventure; all of which were to become the starting points for the *Ideate* stage that was to come next. From all of this, we were also able to conclude that the narrative needed to be open-ended to facilitate a variety of programming and storytelling, and to ignite the imagination.

As we started to think deeper about the design, we considered that the Port would not only be a place of discovery for the young, but also for parents and seniors to rediscover their childhood. We recognised the opportunity for quality time between parents and children, as well as the lasting memories we hoped would emerge from that time. The Port would be a haven for busy dads and moms, a place they could unwind and connect with their kids.

As we were thinking of names for this experience, it dawned on us that many children's books had "lost" in their title! It struck us that children love stumbling upon and searching for something. With that, we put on our seafarer hats and nautical wear and started to imagine an experience that would capture this spirit of adventure and discovery. We dreamed of a port with islands, full of curiosities from a voyage around the world. We imagined secret passwords and daring expeditions with treasures awaiting those who solved these hidden challenges. We called this family experience, "The Port of Lost Wonder: Satisfying Wonder, Curiosity, and Connection."

THAT GOOD FEELING

>>>>>>>>>>>>>>>>>>>>>>>

Your cells start absorbing all
the nutrients and begin to repair
and maintain. Come alive!

AWAKENING

wake, every
nutritionist
educate
us.

>>>>>>>>>>>>>>>>>>>>>>

This creates awareness, new recipes
and new products that will
enlighten the MIND. We want
to wake everyone up.

SOULFUL GOODNESS

>>>>>>>>>>>>>>>>>>>>>>>

Go beyond the Bowl. Your connection
and involvement fuels our passion.
Talk to us on Facebook.

Saladstop is a salad chain based in Singapore. Despite being a relatively young company at the time the project started, it is a successful business with an eye on the future. When the owners wanted to better convey the company's true values and qualities, the ONG&ONG Experience Design studio was brought on board to innovate a new Saladstop customer experience.

While some of us in the studio are salad fans, there's a small group who believes only rice counts as real food. The project was an opportunity for this group to see salads in a new light. *Discovery* was a two-week long journey where we engaged senior management, staff, and suppliers. We also observed and engaged customers at 5 different Saladstop outlets. Some of us ate of a lot of salad in the process and were surprised by how delicious salad could be. Others nibbled at the raw greens and fled to the safe comfort of *char siew* rice and *nasi padang*. All of us had fun learning about a food category that is yet to be well-established and understood in Singapore.

We returned to the studio and synthesised the various interviews and observations. Insights started to surface. When we interviewed the founders individually, there was a common thread. They wanted to go beyond providing excellent service and products to being a role model that inspired healthy living. We were so thrilled with this vision that we decided to create a single narrative for everyone, from staff to customers, to rally around.

As we analysed the interview transcripts and observation notes from the different outlets, we noticed each store had a unique clientele depending on whether it was located in the central business district, the research and development zone or Singapore's main shopping belt. There were subtle but important differences in customer segmentation. This directed us to look closer at the engagement responses, which then revealed the various reasons why customers eat at Saladstop. Some chose it for health and dietary preferences. Others chose it due to time constraints.

BROCCOLI

Very rich in fiber!

Keeps stomach and
digestive systems healthy

Great immune
strengtheners!

Space Planning

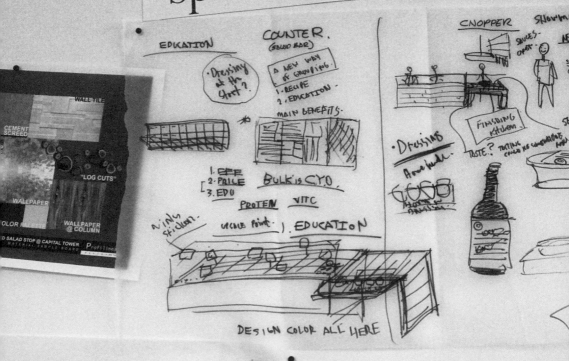

Amidst mounds of paper, *Post-Its* and empty coffee cups, we constructed four archetypical customer personas. We combined these personas with our research on eating experiences and culture in Singapore and around the world. This led to a set of insights that shaped our approach in the later *Ideate* stage.

This methodical process led to innovations at the *Ideate* phase. We now had a clearer narrative and overarching strategy for a more meaningful Saladstop experience.

Synthesis involves looking at gathered information and seeking the logic and order within. Now look back at the project that you are working on. How will you look at the information and data that you have gathered? Do you think you might synthesise your own insights to create truly remarkable experiences? Need more elaboration? Turn the page.

YOUR FAVOURITE SALADS & WRAPS!

INDULGE IN THE BEST SALADS & WRAPS IN TOWN

Tuna San Salad

Omega 3 Baby Wrap

Or Create-Your-Own!

Create-Your-Own salad, wrap or roll! Pick from over 50 fresh salad & topping ingredients, as well as in-house dressings.

SALADSTOP!

JOIN THE SALADSTOP! MOVEMENT AND MAKE A DIFFERENCE

SAVE 29.5 FT² OF RAINFOREST OR WILDLIFE HABITAT SPACE WITH EACH PURCHASE OF THE KINDA SABAH SALAD/WRAP

YOU CAN ALSO DONATE YOUR FREE ITEM SALAD/WRAP FROM PEACE AND LOVE XXL PT

SALADSTOP!

TUNA SAN

OH CRAB LAH!

HAIL CAESAR

IRON "WO" MAN

GO GEISHA

OMEGA 3 BABY!

OUR STORES

Capital Tower
168 Robinson Road #01-05 Singapore 068912

Chevron House
30 Raffles Place #01-36 Singapore 048622

CityLink Mall
One Raffles Link #B1-13 Singapore 039393

Fusionopolis
1 Fusionopolis Way #01-03, IN Connexis, Singapore 138632

Great World City
1 Kim Seng Promenade #01-21A Singapore 237994

Marina Bay Link Mall
8 Marina Boulevard #B2-77/78 Singapore 018981

Novena Square
238 Thomson Road #02-24 Singapore 307683

One George Street
One George Street #01-01, Singapore 049145

PasarBella
200 Turf Club Road #02-K36 Singapore 287994

Suntec City Mall
3 Temasek Boulevard #01-179 Singapore 038983

Takashimaya
391 Orchard Road #B2 07-9-3 Singapore 238873

NYU TISCH School of the Arts Asia
3 Kay Siang Road Singapore 248923

OUR
SYNTHESIS
STEPS

If *Synthesis* seems to you a flurry of activity inside a room lined with post-its from wall to wall, many caffeine-soaked conversations and drawing diagrams that don't seem to make sense, don't fret. We break it down into 5 clear steps. Synthesis can be messy, but if you stick to these 5 steps and trust them, we're confident your team's built-in nose for sense will sniff out some compelling themes and insights.

DOWNLOAD

This is where we present collated
information to each other in a coherent
way. Each member of the team takes
responsibility for his or her area
of focus and gathers and arranges
relevant notes, surveys and interviews.
The output? An easily accessible
databank for the project—usually in
the form of post-its and printout arrays
on foam core boards.

REVIEW

Then we do a collective review of the available information as a team. Each team member presents his findings to others who then offer their own interpretations and comments. At this stage, we start to see many diverse views. The interrogation of the data is often captured on a lot of post-its that can be quickly re-assigned, re-categorized or discarded. We've been told that we account for the largest expenditure of post-its in the whole company.

3

PATTERN

With all the information examined,
verified and debated, we now have
a concise set of data, distilled to a
purer state. Here, we surface recurring
patterns and themes that will form
insights for future stages.

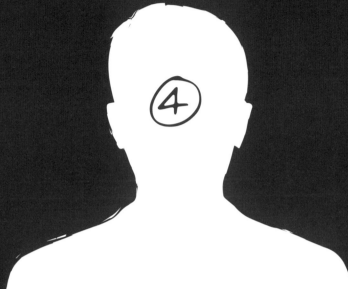

PERSONA

We also create personas to reflect various user groups. Instead of creating a single one-size-fits-all persona, we usually create three to six, with the "extreme" users defining the limits of our strategy. Personas are important pivots in our projects. They tell us who we are designing for, and why we should make certain decisions. Personas ground our decisions and keep us focused.

References
—
[1] *Economist Steven Levitt On Why Data Needs Stories | Co.Create* ., http://www.fastcocreate.com/1683190/economist-steven-levitt-on-why-data-needs-st (accessed June 01, 2015).
[2] *Sentosa Annual Report 13/14, Total Island Guest Arrivals,* http://www.sentosa.gov.sg/sentosaAR13_14/guest_arrivals.html (accessed June 01, 2015).
[3] *Adora Svitak: What Adults Can Learn From Kids | Talk Video | TED.com,* https://www.ted.com/talks/adora_svitak#t-70966 (accessed June 01, 2015).

(5)

NARRATIVE

With all the processing of information
done, we now have enough knowledge
of the project on hand that can be
strung together into a single narrative.
Often only a few sentences long, this
narrative will contain our design strategy.

IDE

Relationships FUEL ideas
ideas
Ideas

ATE

In the future, the battle will change from the designer fighting to be the best, to an integrated world where individuals of different disciplines are committed to getting the absolute best design out of each other.

You've hacked through the dense jungle of Post-its, patiently sought clarity, and now you have your eyes on the treasure. You know where you need to go (that incredible experience in the end), but there is no well-trodden path ahead of you. You need to find a way to get there. *Creatively*. You need to ideate your way out of this. But where do we even start to look for ideas?!

Thankfully, we have the knowledge and insights gathered from *Discovery* and *Synthesis*. Equipped with narratives and stories inspired by the insights, we have guiding lights by which we can navigate the search for ideas.

At this stage of the process, no idea is a bad idea. All suggestions are equally valid. Everyone is encouraged to be at their creative best and to look near and far for inspiration.

Coming up with good and innovative ideas is not easy. At the studio, when we feel stuck in a rut, we've found it useful to take a walk and come back to the problem later. We also look to others before us for inspiration. Steven Johnson's book, *"Where Good Ideas Come From: The Natural History of Innovation"* and its accompanying TED talk are studio favourites. In it, he explores how great minds across time and disciplines— from old-school intellectuals like Darwin and Freud, to new-school technology giants like Google and Apple who develop great ideas. His fascinating exploration may perhaps put things in perspective and inspire you.

"The patterns are simple, but followed together, they make for a whole that is wiser than the sum of its parts. Go for a walk; cultivate hunches; write everything down, but keep your folders messy; embrace serendipity; make generative mistakes; take on multiple hobbies; frequent coffeehouses and other liquid networks; follow the links; let others build on your ideas; borrow, recycle; reinvent. Build a tangled bank."

Steven Johnson
Where Good Ideas Come From:
The Natural History of Innovation

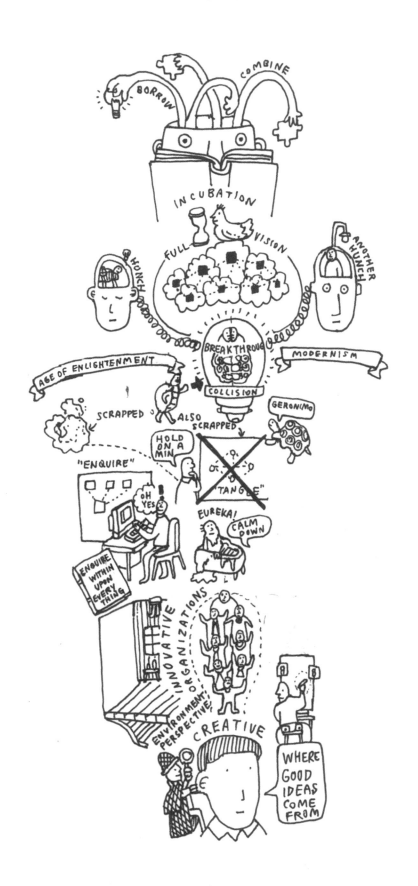

THE CRANES

For a start, let's consider residential buildings, or "houses" as non-architects call them. How does one come up with fresh ideas for those?

The answer lies in how we frame the question. Sometimes, it's easy to forget that architects don't build houses, but homes. While it takes hands to build a house, only hearts can build a home. Our task as experience designers is to make room for that.

The homeowners reading this may agree when we say that home is the only physical space they can truly express themselves. The designer's vision for the building is less relevant than the owner's vision. The owners are, after all, the end-users who will be living in that space for (hopefully) a long while! As experience designers, we take on the responsibility of creating a personal space homeowners feel a deep connection with. Ideally, it'd be a connection so deep they cannot imagine living anywhere else.

To many, home is identity manifest. It is where their personal stories come alive and their aesthetic tastes, quirks, and belongings rest easy, assured of their holding place on the planet. Home is a reflection of the lifestyle they have and the one they aspire towards. In short, home is all at once an incarnatiton of present reality and future dreams.

When we were approached to design this pair of houses, the client shared his vision for it with us:

"Joo Chiat has an eclectic mix of people and it has an extremely local flavour. I want people who live at The Cranes to have an authentic and memorable life experience of this neighbourhood."

We were also told to design for three familial generations. The client cast the vision of a modern kampong. He hoped both tenants and family members would be taken with a spirit of neighbourliness. With that, the narrative for this project emerged naturally – we needed to design "a neighbourhood in a house."

Joo Chiat is a neighbourhood all at once private yet porous, modern and kitschy. It is a place for both the affluent and for the more modestly moneyed. For a final splash of colour, heritage and sleaze live down the street from each other.

As we crafted our ideas, we knew we had to capture this unique *rojak* of character within the house without going overboard with nostalgic elements. The modern lifestyle had to thrive in here. With so many homes to be built in these houses, we had to ensure privacy while providing communal spaces for social activities. We envisioned social impact for both the residents of the houses and the larger neighbourhood. Could The Cranes become an inspiration for the rest of Joo Chiat?

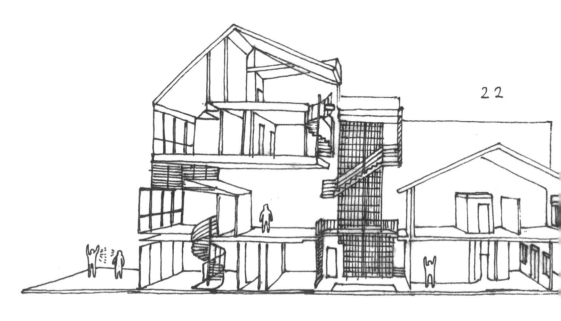

22

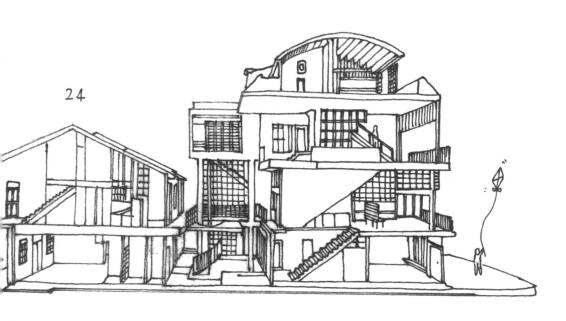

24

The ideation process for this drew on the positive memories of the owners and potential tenants whom we spoke to. We listened to stories of close quarters living—so close everyone saw everything everyone else was doing—without misunderstanding or animosity. We learned of chance meetings on the street and neighbours welcoming each other into their homes with open doors.

With this rich source material, we imagined new stories of community for The Cranes. We created six different houses across three levels and within the envelope of the two shophouse units. "Village squares" and "streets" became the inspiration for architectural devices designed to promote social interaction. The experience of travelling through the house horizontally or vertically became an opportunity for human connection.

Wise men and women before us declared,
"the kitchen is the heart of the home." We
would have been fools to ignore such wisdom.
We channeled our idea-generating energy into
creating an intimate and cosy communal kitchen.
We also felt that chores like laundry didn't have
to be dreadful solitary deeds, but activities to be
enjoyed in friendly company.

We kept to the client's vision and also
designed the Cranes to feel like a warm and
friendly neighbour to the other parts of the
area. We dissolved the boundary between The
Cranes and the rest of Joo Chiat by placing a
communal dining room at one doorstep, and a
sculptural feature wall at another. Both became
neighbourhood magnets, attracting curious
passers-by. We were ecstatic to see house
and neighbourhood become one.

FRANK BY OCBC

If one could use the experience design process to design a house, surely one could also use it to reinvent a Gen-Y banking experience?

Since our target demographic was known more for spending than saving, we started the ideation process with a simple thought:

What if the banking experience felt more like the shopping experience they were familiar with?

say cheese

bi-cycle

HOT PICK

all souped up

fill 'er up

tv land

magic beans

home run

take that!

pucker up

side

sofa so good

purple scooter

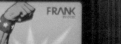
i've got the power

This simple but powerful reframing of the experience led us to rethink everything about banking, leading us to a "shopping" experience where customers picked designs for their customised bank cards. Turning banking from a boring chore into an interactive experience, we introduced opportunities for customers to browse the cards and ask questions about the various banking products, and discuss their banking needs. The space was redesigned to be welcoming and spacious and readily adaptable to mall unit spaces.

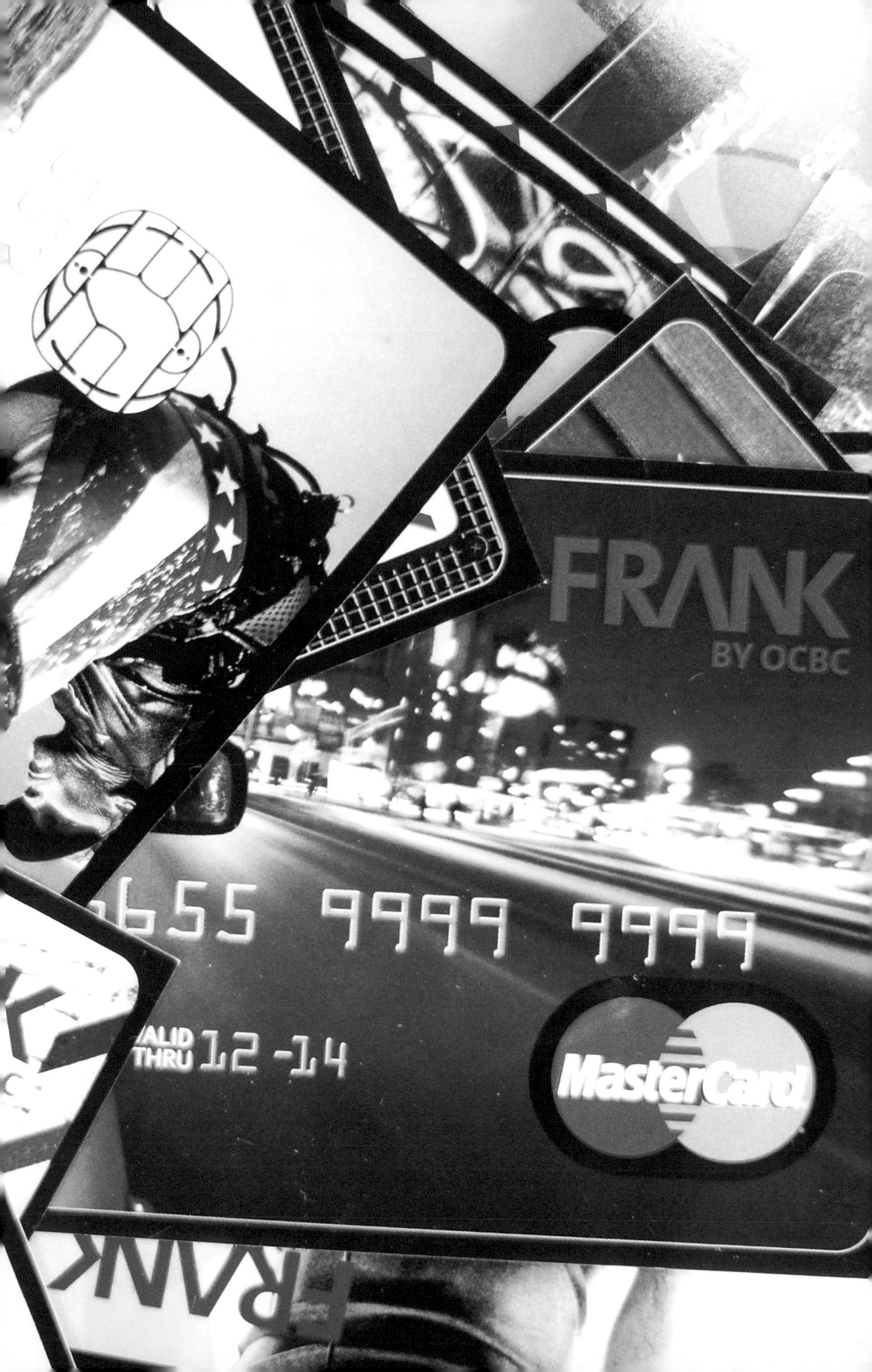
FRANK
BY OCBC
655 9999 9999
VALID THRU 12-14
MasterCard

Whilst creating a customer journey that was fresh, we also started to ask seemingly odd questions. Who is this Bank? What kind of person would this bank be? What would he enjoy? We gave the banking experience a *personality*.

We explored the tone of the bank's voice and went in search of a name that would resonate with the Gen-Y audience. Then, we met FRANK. Honest, sincere, stylish and open, FRANK is unapologetic about being true to his playful self. He made the bank seem human.

FRANK is excited about life and wants to live
it to the fullest. We fell in love straight away
and couldn't wait for everyone to meet him.

From the physical space to the marketing
campaigns and online banking portal,
FRANK poured his personality into every
aspect of the banking experience. With FRANK,
banking was no longer about bank officers
in staid blazers, bad background music,
and gruelling queues. Banking became fun.
And from all we've heard since he warped
into existence, FRANK is a pretty popular guy.

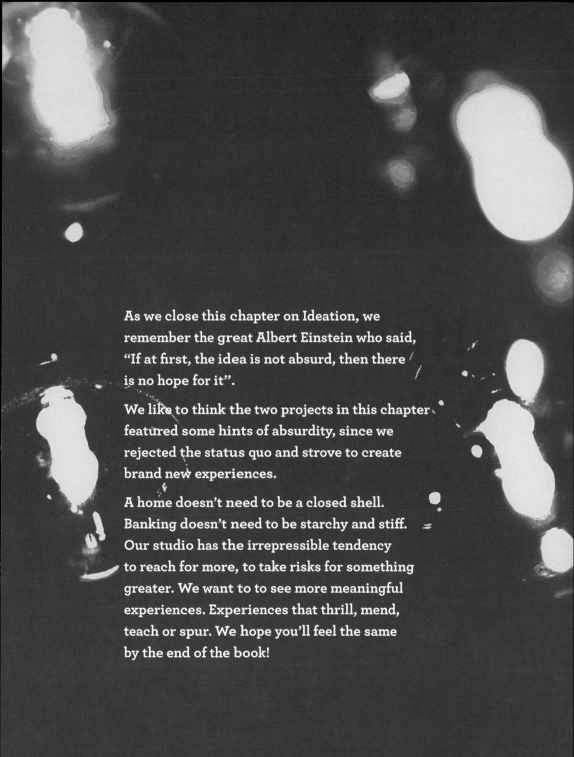

As we close this chapter on Ideation, we remember the great Albert Einstein who said, "If at first, the idea is not absurd, then there is no hope for it".

We like to think the two projects in this chapter featured some hints of absurdity, since we rejected the status quo and strove to create brand new experiences.

A home doesn't need to be a closed shell. Banking doesn't need to be starchy and stiff. Our studio has the irrepressible tendency to reach for more, to take risks for something greater. We want to to see more meaningful experiences. Experiences that thrill, mend, teach or spur. We hope you'll feel the same by the end of the book!

OUR
IDEATION
IDEAS

Ideation can be chaotic, but it is precisely this chaos that lets different voices collide and combine into truly novel solutions. There is no one way to do this, but here are a few of our key guiding principles that perhaps can help you along.

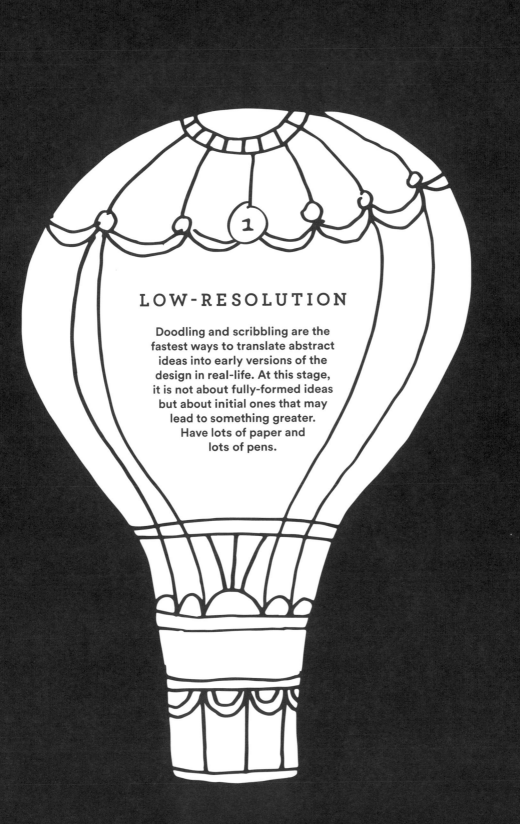

LOW-RESOLUTION

Doodling and scribbling are the fastest ways to translate abstract ideas into early versions of the design in real-life. At this stage, it is not about fully-formed ideas but about initial ones that may lead to something greater. Have lots of paper and lots of pens.

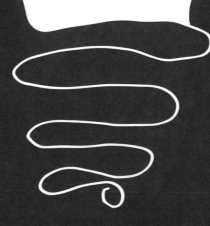

LET IT FLOW

We like letting ideas take on a life of their own. We stay open to possibilities, comments and critique. We try not to judge things prematurely, preferring a full bag of options till ideas eliminate themselves or are tested and found wanting.

3

MORE IS MORE

The point of this phase is to generate a ton of ideas. This is the time to let your creativity flow and allow for volume and variety in your ideas. There will be time later for evaluating these ideas but for now, let the sheer number of ideas reign supreme.

4

KEEP IT SIMPLE, NOT SIMPLISTIC

Good ideas are often deceptively simple and easy to understand, even if rich and complex. Having said that, don't settle for the obvious. Peek past the horizon. What lies there?

5

TOUCHPOINTS

Anything can be the starting
point for the creation of an
amazing experience. Spatial
proportions, spatial sequences,
materials, lights, sound, smells
and any other sensorial element
could do the trick. Let these
inspire you. Think deep on them.
Repurpose them. Turn them on
their heads. Build something
that surprises even you.

References
—
[1]   Where Good Ideas Come From
Quotes by Steven Johnson, http://www.
goodreads.com/work/quotes/12645873-
where-good-ideas-come-from-the-nat
(accessed June 01, 2015).
[2]   Ray Oldenburg, The great good
place: cafés, coffee shops, bookstores,
bars, hair salons, and other hangouts at
the heart of a community. (Washington:
Marlowe & Company, 1999)

PROT

TYPE

FAIL FAST, LEARN QUICK!

Failure is ironically
one of the greatest
tools that helps
us think.

After Ideation, the question we ask is: which are the good ideas? Sometimes it's hard to tell. That's one of the main functions of *Prototype*—to help us test ideas in the real world so we can watch users reactions and gauge the accuracy of our assumptions.

For instance, it was reported that the first Apple Watch prototype was an iPhone with a velcro strap. Not elegant, and likely clumsy. However, it would have allowed designers and engineers to test software and study human interaction with the device.

Prototypes fall into two categories: rapid prototyping and pilots, or technical prototypes. As explained by David Aycan and Paolo Lorenzoni in a Harvard Business Review article[2], rapid prototyping aims for quantity over quality. Dozens of sketches, wireframes, enacted service scenarios, and Play-Doh models are created quickly to get a feel for ideas. On the other end of the spectrum are pilots and technical prototypes, which generally aim to get as close as possible to the "right" answer in full fidelity. In the ONG&ONG Experience Design Studio, we favour rapid prototyping.

If you thought some of the ideas you had were risky, this prototyping stage of the experience design process is the opportunity to check for seaworthiness. If you thought you had a sure-win/knockout idea, *Prototype* is also the chance to prove it! It's where we get actual feedback from users and stakeholders on realised ideas so we know how to refine them.

Let's see how some *Prototype* sessions went. Were our assumptions correct? Did the ideas produce the intended effects? What did we learn?

BLOODBANK@WOODLANDS BY HSA

BLOODBANK @WOODLANDS

We picked up other lessons from the past, and were especially struck by the fond memories people had of getting a steaming cup of Milo after donating blood. It was a simple and powerful interaction, one we decided to keep.

In 2010, we were tasked to design a new satellite Blood Bank centre at Woodlands Civic Centre, which was to be known as Bloodbank@ Woodlands. We set out to create a new blood donation experience by applying our process.

The champion donors taught us a lot. We learned their primary motivation was simply to help society and others. All these donors wanted was appreciation, not gifts.

This led us to introduce elements from the Red Cross marketing campaign that highlighted the number of lives saved and had small notes of appreciation placed at form-filling booths. We also spotted an opportunity to reduce the anxiety of first-time donors by making a clearer introduction to the blood donation experience.

This led us to propose the use of graphics in the waiting room to evoke a sense of accomplishment and assurance. We picked up other lessons from the past, and were especially struck by the fond memories people had of getting a steaming cup of *Milo* after donating blood. It was a simple and powerful interaction, one we decided to keep.

The self-help refreshment station allows donors to grab a bite after their donation. These seats are modular and movable. The graphic wall explains what happens to their blood and lets them know their contributions are appreciated.

The firm-filling booths can be made collapsible to provide extra space in times of emergency blood drives.

The old waiting area used to be made up of rows of chairs – the new waiting area is more informal and inviting, while able to accommodate more people.

James, 57
Saved 354 lives
Yoga Centre Owner
Champion Blood Donor

Special notes at the form-filling booth reminds donors that their contribution is valued and encourage them to come back as repeated donors.

You are saving 3 lives

Honesty is blood safety

A workshop with the staff brought to our attention various recommendations to improve the experience . These were grouped by the four main stages in the blood donation experience—registration, medical screening and blood testing, blood donation, and post-donation. Recommendations ranged from the kind of background music, to the lighting of the space. They included operational ideas such as having staff members walk first-time donors through each station to put them at ease.

We found that there was a preference for a clean and warm space with a natural palette of green, wood, and white. Someone even proposed an idea to throw a quick birthday party for donors who donated on their birthday!

These ideas were compacted, refined and melded with our data from *Discovery* and *Synthesis* and then translated into an initial layout of the new Blood Bank experience.

We began the prototyping session by giving Blood Bank staff an overview of the new layout. We explained the rationale for each design decision and followed with a physical walkthrough. We showed them the various graphic ideas and the moods we wanted to evoke for the different sectors. To better communicate the intent of the ideas, we role-played the first-time donor. As they watched, the staff gave even more feedback on their needs at each section, allowing us to obtain more useful data.

The materials used included cardboard boxes, pull-up banners and whatever movable furniture was at our disposal. Foldable chairs, whiteboards and ice-boxes were recruited to mock up the essential spatial touchpoints of the experience. It was light, cheap and fast.

Staff were invited to walk through the various spaces and interact with the key touchpoints. Because the furniture was movable, the staff from the Blood Bank could shift pieces around to test other solutions. We plied them with questions and recorded their responses, which further clarified the steps we would take to improve the design.

Without the benefit of the staff's cumulative knowledge regarding day-to-day operations, we would not have learned some important things. The Blood Bank staff even suggested a modular console for their information counter. In the event the Bank had to be transformed into an emergency blood donation centre, the modular console could be easily moved to create more room. Aside from valuable "insider knowledge", we got feedback on the new touchpoints, such as the "community wall" designed to connect the Blood Bank to the contributions of the community. With the help of our Blood Bank friends and experts, we became more confident we were on our way to a better blood donation experience.

	REGULAR 12oz	LARGE 16oz	X-LARGE 20oz
Hot Chocolate			
Iced Chocolate	5.20	5.70	6.20
Hot Vanilla	5.50	6.00	6.50
Iced Vanilla	5.20	5.70	6.20
	5.30	5.80	6.30

YOUR CREATIVE OPTION

Add a shot

Add a flavour 0.80
Caramel, Hazelnut, Cocoa powder, Chai powder, 0.70
Dairy-free Vanilla powder

Add soy milk
US organic soy milk 0.30

As a player in the highly competitive coffee landscape in Singapore, Spinelli recognised an innovative experience would differentiate it from the crowd. Many of our case studies showed that consumers today expect authenticity and good service. We sought to craft new experiences and systems that would address these needs.

Discovery included a range of workshops, in-depth interviews, store observations and case study analyses. A few key staff and customer insights emerged to help us shape the brand DNA and story, which helped us to navigate the later parts of the process. Then, in a few caffeine-powered Ideation sessions, we discussed options and ideas to differentiate the Spinelli experience. Ideas ranged from new graphic communication strategies to physical improvements and operational procedures. Excited that we had something great on our hands, we had to find out if it would all work. Hence, we prototyped the new experience..

The Spinelli branches at China Square Central and Wheelock Place were selected as prototype venues for their different customer profiles. Each prototype session lasted just two hours, taking place at relatively busy periods of the day. Both were set up to test specific ideas. Back at the studio, we analysed our results across sessions in light of our hypotheses. Knowing exactly what we were testing for made prototyping an especially effective innovation tool.

We tested different customer journeys for ordering with simple foam boards, print-outs and rearranged pieces of furniture. To measure the impact of these prototypes, we observed the customers' reactions to the new experience and conducted surveys with customers and staff.

Like *Discovery* and *Synthesis,* we studied
the comments on the various aspects of the
prototype. Qualitative and quantitative data
were collated and analysed while the critique
and comments were metabolised for the final
design stage. Each tested idea received a grade:
keep, rethink or refine. Then, we put the results
on a dashboard for easy reference.

The innovation of new experiences means that we
are often dealing with untested ideas, touchpoints
and processes. Prototypes gather feedback for
these. Mock-ups and simulation exercises give
us clues to refinement while keeping costs low.

With multiple sensorial touchpoints in an
experience, prototype sessions communicate
complex ideas simply and succinctly to
stakeholders. They do it better than photo-
realistic renderings or videos because you get
to interact with them.

OUR PROTOTYPE PRO-TIPS

Like everything else in the experience design process, there is no right or wrong way of running a prototype. You know your project best. Change it up any way you want! In any case, here are a few things that might help you along, especially if you're running your first ever prototype.

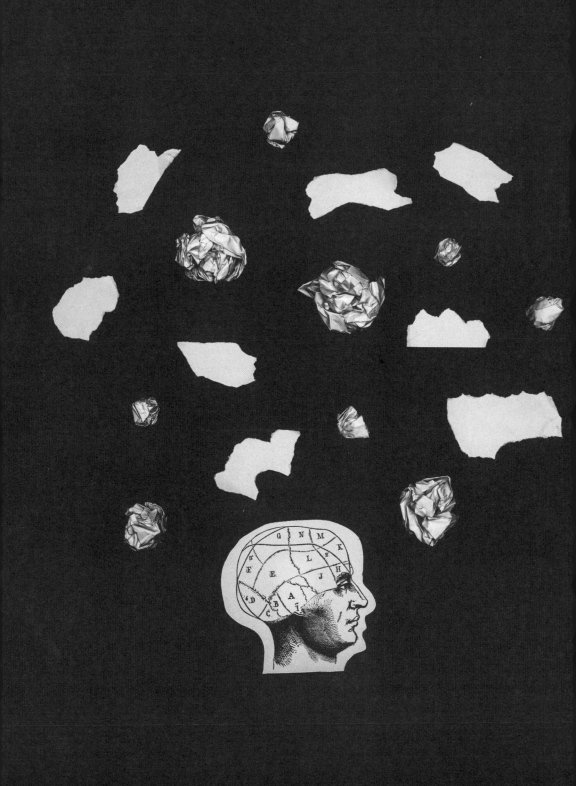

KEEP IN MIND

What you are trying to test - Set your own expectations right. A prototype is designed to test very specific ideas in a controlled environment and should not be expected to do everything very well. If you are clear on what you're testing, the prototyping session will be simpler and more accurate.

HELP USERS AND STAKEHOLDERS VISUALISE

Because a prototype is not the full representation of an idea, explain the rationale and the ideas behind the exercise to everyone who is involved. If people share a common understanding, ideas can be appreciated more fully and better feedback can be gathered.

FAIL FAST

Because you are testing specific ideas, there is a
chance that some of these will fail, so embrace it!
We recommend failing fast so that you may quickly
iterate a better version. The more ideas you test,
the sooner weak ones are weeded out, leaving the
stronger ones. There is even a book titled "'Fail Fast,
Fail Often: How Losing Can Help You Win"!

A PROTOTYPE MUST BE LIGHT, CHEAP & QUICK

If you're going to be failing fast (see previous point), then you want your prototype to be quickly adjustable and almost disposable. Find ways to achieve the desired impact in a low-cost manner. You will see in the later pages that our prototypes sometimes just entail cardboard and simple print-outs. This is quick and useful for testing ideas.

OBSERVE & MEASURE

While doing a prototyping exercise is a load of fun, always remember that there is a purpose to all of this (see point 1). With that, make sure you are always observing how people use your prototype. Measure the relevant metrics and take all of this in as you return to refine the idea. Take lots of photos and videos, conduct interviews and listen to what everyone has to say.

References
—

[1] *Iphone Killer: The Secret History Of The Apple Watch by David Pierce* - http://www.wired.com/2015/04/the-apple-watch/ (accessed June 01, 2015).
[2] *The Future of Prototyping Is Now Live - HBR,* https://hbr.org/2014/03/the-future-of-prototyping-is-now-live/ (accessed June 01, 2015).

DES

IGN

PEOPLE > PORTFOLIO

More than just fashioning beauty, designing an experience is the ability to create quality connections between people, places and technology.

We've mentioned narratives a lot and as we near the end of the book, you may have noticed that designing experiences is a bit like writing stories.

A delightful experience is not very different from a good story. Engaging experiences go beyond mere transportation of a person from one point in space to another. They take him on a multi-sensory journey. To the untrained eye, the elements that make up an experience may be imperceptible. On closer inspection, you will see how all its parts contribute. Textures and shapes, sounds and the sequencing of spaces all add to the overall spatial experience.

We hope the pages before this showed you a new way of approaching your projects. Starting from the project brief, the experience design process leads us deep into the minds of customers and stakeholders. It's a meditative truth-finding odyssey. It's a daring dive into a sea of ideas, safe and strange. It's a romp into the imagination through the portal of prototype places and services. We hope this 5-stage journey offered you new perspectives and an appreciation for design not unlike what Paul Theroux wrote,
"You go away for a long time and return a different person – you never come all the way back."

You've taken a peek at how to design experiences. Now, we want to tell you stories of the spaces we created so you can experience design. So, find yourself a good drink and get comfortable in your chair. We hope you enjoy these stories! ENJOY...

HDB PUNGGOL BRANCH

The excitement of moving into a new home is still buzzing in him. The pieces of furniture are in and all that is left are a few minor repairs to get his first HDB flat up and running. Being a first-time homeowner, everything is new to Eric, and something as simple as purchasing a Season Parking Ticket for his car is a fresh new experience. He does not want to take any chances with the online application and decides that heading down to the HDB Punggol Branch would be the best way to get his transaction done properly.

Upon reaching the Punggol Branch, Eric is pleased to see that it is a contrast from the one he followed his parents to as a child. The materials and lighting make it warm and comfortable with clear and well-designed signage adding to the

positive experience. He recalls the poster he saw a couple of days back about the Branch piloting a new customer service experience that would better meet residents' needs. Then, he notices the Roving Ambassador, who is standing attentively near the e-lobby. Eric feels assured and knows that this is going to be easier than he had imagined.

Eric walks over to her and explains that he came to apply for a new Season Parking Ticket. The Roving Ambassador politely assists him to obtain a queue number by scanning his identity card before directing him to the waiting area that seems particularly busy today.

The Community Wall is showing upcoming events in the neighbourhood on its integrated screen, but Eric is more interested in the other wall that has colourful graphics on it. As he approaches it, he sees that it is a wall filled with useful hints about what can be done at the Branch and on the HDB website, all categorised and colour-coded. The simple infographics also draw him in, inviting him to understand some of the processes that have so far been completely alien to him.

As he waits for his turn, he sees how the various HDB staff are focused and confident while assisting their customers. Looking around, he also notices how much care and thought has been put into designing a physical environment that supports the various transactions at the Branch. He breaks into a slight smile as he observes a little girl being engaged at the dedicated kid's corner of the family service counter.

"HDB has really taken the effort to train their staff so that they are able to provide a more personable service. I can see that a lot of work has gone on behind the scenes," he thinks to himself.

His number comes up, and Eric walks straight across the carpeted floor to the counter that he was assigned to. As he approaches, the aide stands up and welcomes him. "Hello Mr Lee, please have a seat," she says. "I see here from the records that it's the first time you're applying for a

Season Parking Ticket?" Then, after hearing more details from Eric, the counter staff hits a few keys on her keyboard and turns the monitor around to face him.

"Actually Mr Lee, you can apply for this at home. We use the same system to do this. Here, let me show you," says the aide. They continue to chat and complete the transaction in less than 10 minutes. "That was a breeze. Thanks!" says Eric as he gets up, shakes the hand of the aide and makes his way out of the Punggol Branch. On the way out, he decides to make a short detour to the Compliments Wall to leave a message of thanks to the staff for making his visit simple and painless.

SINGAPORE BOTANIC GARDENS SHOPS

It has been a sunny and uplifting afternoon and Niki's visit to the Botanic Gardens today has been nothing short of amazing. No wonder the Gardens were listed in so many international websites as the place to visit in Singapore.

It was memorable day spent walking along the meandering paths and appreciating the thousands of species on display, all the while spending time with the family. True to what she read, the Gardens are indeed a living heritage where every leaf, blade of grass and flower expresses life. Niki wanted to bring a piece of this back home to share with her loved ones.

One of the Botanic Gardens staff had told her about the gift shops around the Gardens – one at the Nassim Gate and one at the other Tanglin Gate. She had read somewhere that the shops had been designed differently, and considered dropping by after her first round of souvenir shopping.

Niki's smile widened, as she stepped into the air-conditioned space. More than offering respite from the tropical heat, it was the lightness and beauty of the shop that captured her heart in an instant. The textured white bricks and floor tiles hinted at Singapore's colonial heritage and the patterned fabric wall panels together with a selection of fresh orchids around the shop felt like a natural extension of the rest of the garden. Niki moved towards the Orchid Bar in the middle of the room, drawn to the range of products inspired by Singapore's national flower. Jewellery, perfumes, lotions and even tea were on display, all of which seemed perfect as souvenirs and gifts. The soft lighting in the shop made everything look so good – someone had taken great care in curating the products in the store.

Surrounded by warm recycled timber shelving, vintage clothes racks and artisanal wall sconces, Niki basked in the natural beauty and elegance of the space as she browsed the shelves for gifts. In search of something for everyone, she spent a lot of time at the stationery section, picking out wrapping papers and notebooks in floral patterns and antique biological sketch prints.

Niki could have spent an hour there, but her
husband was beckoning her to pay for her haul.
As she waited in line for her turn at the counter,
she admired the Heritage Wall behind it, mentally
recalling the snippets of information and history
that she had learnt around the garden. She started
to think about which of these artworks and
heritage photographs on display she should get
for her best friend and wondered where she would
hang this at home. She eventually settled on the
photo of Burkill Hall. She knew it would look
perfect near her dining table.

Upon making her payment, the lady at the counter
handed her a story tag and explained that the tag
told the Botanic Gardens' story. Niki thought it
was a lovely idea. With the invitation to write her
own story on the tag, she wrote: "Wish you could
be here with me to see all these beautiful flowers.
Love, Niki."

145 NEIL ROAD

The morning light reflected off the water, sending shimmering streaks of sunshine on the bright blue walls. The ornate centrepiece and carved relief wall panels glowed in the sun, enjoying their new lease of life since the restoration works were completed. The open-to-sky courtyard of this conserved shophouse breathed life into the adjacent spaces.

Everywhere around the house, the past was celebrated in vintage glory. The original timber window screens and many of the floor tiles remained in place, decades after they were first installed. A calligraphic panel and the metal gate found new life in locations around the house. She recalled how layer upon layer, the old paint was stripped to reveal the authentic and striking blue tone of the façade and internal courtyard that mesmerise her every day. As she looked across the length of the house, she started to imagine the scenes that these timber floors and textured bricks must have witnessed over the years. She was pleased that the request of its original owner–that the heritage and history of the property be preserved—had been fulfilled twenty years on.

In her brief to the designers, she had asked for a place where she could feel like she had lived in all her life. A house with soul, it would be an extension of her personality and a place of rest.

Neil Road was busy this morning but within the haven of her conserved shophouse, there was peace. In her space, the building's past and her own future coexisted harmoniously, as though it had always been that way. There was little to suggest the house had been leased for twenty years before it became her first home.

This was undoubtedly a modern dwelling. The new had respectfully found a quiet spot in the old with the extension at the back. No one would have guessed it was new. Just beyond the new island unit in the kitchen, a sweeping, curved red-brick wall terminated the vista. Hiding behind it was the new spiral staircase that led to the roof terrace.

The architects had managed to elegantly blend the character and spatial quality of the past for her to enjoy. She felt so grateful and appreciative of this.

A sudden rustling coming from the top of the staircase broke her meditative state. "Must be the dog," she thought to herself. She got up from the chair, picked up her iPad from the antique table along the pathway and walked across the room to sit at the foot of the new metal staircase. Sitting down, she directed her attention to the glass window at the front of her house.

Peeking through it and past the conserved timber shutters, she saw a beautiful, sunny day outside. It made her remember the architect of her house, who had passionately pointed out how the restored green Chinese awning tiles and the friezes adorned with ceramic chips at the shophouse's façade would glisten in the bright sunshine. She loved the care and effort put into retaining the character and rich Peranakan heritage of the building.

This was truly more than just a house to her. It was a home. A home where old memories keep company with new ones.

SIA KRISFLYER LOUNGE

Every time Ken finds himself at the airport, the voiceover from the movie Love Actually comes to mind, "Whenever I get gloomy with the state of the world, I think about the arrivals gate". It goes on to tell of the happy reunion of lovers, families and friends before ending with, "I've got a sneaky feeling you'll find that love actually is all around." As he strode across the carpeted floors of the airport to catch the long flight home, the words seemed apt.

In the distance, he could see the unmistakable screen of the Singapore Airlines Krisflyer Lounge entrance –always a comforting sight in any city. He headed straight for it with haste. As he walked through the RFID-enabled automatic doors and took the first steps into the foyer, he caught a whiff of kaffir leaves, a familiar scent that transported him home in an instant. "Good afternoon Mr Stevens, and welcome to the Lounge," said the host warmly. A smile appeared on his face.

He wasn't flying First Class today, so he headed the other way and walked past the travel concierge who was helping another passenger with some seat change requests. From what he overheard, it seemed that the passenger was going to be very happy he got his way. He exchanged smiles with another nearby concierge.

The wall of curated art pieces at the Gallery looked majestic. Light fell beautifully on the glazed surfaces of the porcelain pieces. The dotted Peranakan artwork reminded him of a piece he owned, but Ken was hungry. He wanted a bite before taking a closer look at the art and magazines.

Images of Singaporean delights and ingredients whetted his appetite. Settled into a seat at the

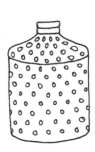
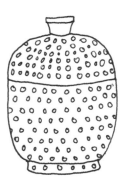

Island Counter, he scanned the menu that was thoughtfully broken into four categories. "Warm & Comforting seems like a good way to nourish the body and soul," he thought.

The Chef was chatty and over lunch, conversation about the differences between Singapore heritage food and hawker food drew a few interested parties around the table, proving food can make the world a little bit smaller. It also made him really excited to get home, but he still had a bit of time to go before boarding.

After his meal, as some of the guests who got involved in that conversation headed to the Bench for a drink and to continue their discussion on Singaporean food, he decided to head to the Living Room. He gravitated to the luxuriously finished SIA chair to write in his journal. Nestled in the plush chair, he adjusted the lighting, slipped into a reflective mood and began to transcribe his thoughts. The host offered him a drink, but he politely declined and continued writing. The soft music playing in the background lulled him into deep focus, though another guest was taking a power-nap to these tunes.

Before long, it was five minutes to boarding time.
A pit stop to the bathroom was in order
so he could prepare for the long flight ahead.
He changed into a comfortable pair of shoes and
ensured all was in place while keeping an eye on
the clock in the bathroom.

With everything done, he headed across the
Lounge and was greeted once more by the host,
who checked to ensure he was ready to board.
He was also informed that other SIA staff would
attend to him if he needed anything else.
He thanked them for their attentiveness.
But now, it was time to go home.

What about the effect of experience design on business outcomes? We might interview dozens of people and spend hundreds of hours puzzling over a design problem, but can the process *really* change things for the better?

We know it can. Experience design is a tested method for creating real business impact. It generates new ways of doing things. It sets new standards. Don't take our word for it. Here's what our clients and other sources had to say about the work.

SALADSTOP
Winner of SG Mark 2014

Before we helped to transform it, SaladStop was just about the sale of its product—salad. Today, it is a more complete service experience that invites customers to join a healthy-eating movement. Within three months, outlets that incorporated the new identity and spatial design saw a significant increase of 10-15% in customer footfall. SaladStop was a winner of the SG Mark 2014.

In the words of Adrien Desbaillets, President and Director of SaladStop, *"The customer feedback has been fantastic. A lot of people find it a lot more warm and welcoming. They feel a lot more comfortable. They have also been able to resonate with the brand and connect with SaladStop. We've seen a boost in revenue we feel is directly associated with the branding."*

FRANK by OCBC
Banking & Payment Trailblazer Awards 2012, Smart Card Awards Asia 2012, Financial Insights Innovation Award 2013, BAI-Finacle Global Banking Innovation Awards 2013, SG Mark 2014

When FRANK launched, the Financial Brand called it "maybe the coolest bank Gen-Y has ever seen." In an interview with The Straits Times, Head of FRANK by OCBC Mark Leong reported that "assets under management in OCBC's

youth segment [had] multiplied six-fold since the
FRANK programme was launched in 2011", and
that "revenue from the bank's youth segment also
tripled last year (2014), compared with the year
before." He added that "the FRANK savings
account is the most popular product under the
FRANK programme, with take-up rates growing
35 per cent year-on-year."

http://business.asiaone.com/news/ocbcs-efforts-woo-young-adults-frank-pay

HDB PUNGGOL BRANCH
FutureGov Award 2014 (Service Innovation)

In 2014, the Housing & Development Board (HDB)
won the international FutureGov Awards 2014
(Service Innovation) for creating a new and
improved customer experience at its Punggol
Branch Office. The award is an international
benchmark for public sector innovation.

The new branch office did not just win professional
acclaim. It also won the hearts of citizens and
residents in the Punggol neighbourhood. In an
HDB survey conducted on Punggol residents in
2013, more than 90% liked the warm and engaging
environment in the Branch. Writing in his blog
after visiting the Punggol Branch Office, Minister
for National Development Khaw Boon Wan
referred to the new changes, saying, "These are
small changes, but what a difference they make."

https://mndsingapore.wordpress.com/2013/02/28/
new-branch-new-opportunity-new-customer-experience/
http://www.hdb.gov.sg/fi10/fi10296p.nsf/PressReleas-
es/6A7A5561A9AE0BAE48257D700002F84F?OpenDocument

PORT OF LOST WONDER BY SENTOSA (POLW)

Sam Lee, Leisure Management Director at Sentosa shared in an interview: "The impact was something we never imagined. Within the span of five months, Sentosa and POLW had 54,000 children visiting. That doesn't even include the parents, which would make it about 150,000 guests. We have doubled our revenue targets. In terms of annual membership, we hit our target of 1000 new members three weeks after opening. Because of that, we had no choice [but] to stop accepting new memberships."

Since then, POLW has opened its doors to about 250,000 children, with visitor numbers over the past three years estimated at 3 to 4 million including parents. In this time, POLW has made approximately $7.5 million in revenue.

BLOODBANK@WOODLANDS BY HSA

The opening of Bloodbank@Woodlands marked a significant milestone in the Health Sciences Authority's (HSA) mission to secure and manage the national blood supply. It is the first fixed satellite blood collection centre, part of a longer-term strategy to integrate blood donation with communities and to make it more convenient.

The second fixed satellite blood collection centre opened at Dhoby Xchange in 2012 using the same design guidelines. In an interview with The Straits Times, HSA reported that the centre has "exceeded expectations with young blood donors making up almost 40 per cent of donor turnout." Figures from HSA also show that the pool of blood donors has grown by 17 per cent from 2008 to 70,855 in 2012.

http://yourhealth.asiaone.com/content/more-youth-donors-downtown-blood-bank

http://www.hsa.gov.sg/content/hsa/en/News_Events/Press_Releases/2011/hsa_launches_1st_satellite.html

Some other awards we've won:

SINGAPORE AIRLINES SILVERKRIS LOUNGE
SG Mark 2014 Platinum,
Golden Pin Award 2015,
Sydney Good Design Awards 2015

STOCK EXCHANGE OF SINGAPORE
International Design Awards 2014

HOUSE AT 145 NEIL ROAD
Urban Redevelopment Authority Heritage
Award 2014 (Residential)

Firm Profile

ONG&ONG DESIGN PROFILE

With a track record of more than four decades in the industry, ONG&ONG has earned an unparalleled reputation for integrating skilled architecture, clever interior design and creative landscape design. Our success lies in the high level of creativity, excellence and commitment we provide to our clients. We continually strive to uphold our mission to be the designer of our age – a premier design practice both locally and in the region. Currently operating in 13 cities, we are managing projects in 18 countries spread over three continents.

Partnering with our clients in their race to the top, ONG&ONG now offers a complete 360° solution – i.e. a parcelled cross-discipline integrated solution, encompassing all aspects of the construction business. We offer a three-pronged 360° solution; namely 360° Design + 360° Engineering + 360° Management. 360° Design encompasses urban planning, architecture, landscape, interior, lighting and brand engagement. 360° Engineering offers civil, structural, electrical, mechanical, fire safety and environmental engineering. 360° Management provides development, project, construction, cost and place management.

In addition to projects in Singapore, ONG&ONG has also completed large-scale developments regionally. This has prompted the setting up of offices in China, Vietnam, India, Malaysia, USA, Indonesia, Mongolia and most recently in Myanmar and Philippines. In-depth knowledge of the local context, culture and regulations allow us to better understand our clients' needs. We are an ISO14001 certified practice and consistently strive to meet and exceed our clients' expectations.

Studio Profile

ONG&ONG EXPERIENCE DESIGN STUDIO

ONG&ONG Experience Design was founded on the understanding that beautiful physical environments alone do not always equate successful experiences, but great experiences are an empathetic and innovative combination of places, people, and technology coming together as a compelling story.

The studio works with clients to establish its story and strategy for memorable experiences that emotionally engage its users and impacts culture. The studio provides a collective integrated expertise across architecture, interior design, brand creation, communication design, service design, film and story, framed by a design thinking approach centered on understanding human motivation and behaviour.

Partners

MARK WEE,
Director, Experience Design, ONG&ONG

Mark Wee is the Director of the ONG&ONG Experience Design studio.
He is an architect, artist, and design thinker. His architectural projects
have also won design awards such as the URA Heritage Award, Singapore
Institute of Architects Design Award, the Interior Design Confederation
(Singapore) Award, and the nation's most prestigious President's Design
Award, amongst others. He has also represented Singapore at the Venice
Architectural Biennale in 2008, the world's oldest and most prestigious
architectural exhibition.

Mark has also coached numerous private and public sector organisations
on using design thinking to solve difficult challenges, ranging from policy
issues, to building innovation cultures, rethinking educational approaches,
and even training future government leaders to be more empathetic.

He studied architecture at Cornell University, and also speaks and teaches
regularly on both architectural design, design thinking,
and service innovation.

KEN YUKTASEVI
Director, Experience Design, ONG&ONG

Ken Yuktasevi is the Co-Director of the ONG&ONG Experience Design
studio. He is a designer, artist and cultural entrepreneur.
He specialises in the field of experiential design, working across the fields
of architecture, interior design, branding and organisational
transformation. He studied arts and design at Stowe College in the UK
where he received the Roxburough Prize for Architecture. He then received
a BA in film and cinematography at Bond University in Australia.

His passion for telling human stories on celluloid compelled him to recreate
that experience in 3D space. This began during his directorship in Leo
International Design Group, and later at UNION Experience which he
founded with Mark Wee in 2006. Yuktasevi's projects include Singapore
Airlines, OCBC Bank, the Singapore Stock Exchange, The Coffee Bean &
Tea Leaf and the Kempinski Hotel in Moscow.

Project Teams

THE CRANES: Adrian Ong, Ken Tan, Daisuke Chew, Mark Teo, Trina Tay, Ren Hui | **145 NEIL ROAD:** Ewan Wong | **SALADSTOP:** Abigail Wong, Ziqq, Joanne Tan, Davina Tjandra | **SIA SILVERKRIS LOUNGE:** Joshua Teo, Abigail Wong, Ho Ren Yung, Stephanie Choo, Natalie Louey *(In collaboration with Awaken group)* Antonia Nichols, So-Young Kang | **PORT OF LOST WONDER BY SENTOSA:** Jan Lim, Trina Tay, Natalie Louey *(In collaboration with Awaken group)* Antonia Nichols, So-Young Kang | **SINGAPORE BOTANIC GARDENS SHOPS:** Stephanie Choo, Reuben Png, Jan Lim, Joanne Sim, Ziqq, Daniel Lee, Trina Tay, Ken Tan | **SPINELLI:** Stephanie Choo, Joanne Sim, Abigail Wong, Daniel Lee, Benjamin Lee, Jaypee Mendoza | **HDB PUNGGOL BRANCH:** Joshua Teo, Jan Lim, Brandon Liu (SCA), Rommel Baluyut (SCA), Benson Chua (SCA) *(In collaboration with Awaken group)* So-Young Kang, David Mervyn Khoo, Luke Chua | **FRANK, OCBC:** Joshua Teo, Trina Tay, Jun Vingson, Kang Shan Shan | **BLOOD BANK:** Joshua Teo, Daisuke Chew

Photographers

BAI JIWEN
Singapore Botanic Gardens Shops, Spinelli

JAUME ALBERT MARTI
Saladstop, The Cranes

SEE CHEE KEONG
145 Neil Road, Port of Lost Wonder by Sentosa

MASANO KAWANA
The Cranes

DEREK SWALWELL
SIA SilverKris Lounge, Sydney

JOVIAN LIM
FRANK by OCBC

DAISUKE CHEW
HDB Punggol Branch